The INVESTING 101 Series

1 Million in 1 Year

Your Easy Guide to 1 Million Dollars in 1 Year or Less

ERICK WALK

CONTENTS

Introduction

PART 1 - How Can You Live Off One Million

    Chapter 1 –   2
    The Elusive Million
    Chapter 2 –   8
    The Millionaire Mindset
    Chapter 3 –   15
    The Four Percent Rule

PART 2 - Making One Million in One Year

    Chapter 4 –   25
    Real Estate
    Chapter 5 –   45
    Stocks
    Chapter 6 –   66
    Forex
    Chapter 7 –   95
    Precious Metals

PART 3 - Writing Your One-Year Plan to Earn 1 Million

    Chapter 8 –   104
    How to Write an Investment Plan
    Chapter 9 –   108
    Your One-Year Plan

Conclusion   113

Introduction

Although one million dollars is not worth as much as it used to, for most people it still represents a "magic number" to aspire to when it comes to saving money. After all, there is still a certain cache in being known as a millionaire, even though the term itself has become heavily devalued. The good news, however, is that most financial experts believe that, these days, one million dollars is a feasible savings goal and that you can retire on this amount, although you won't enjoy a plush and luxurious lifestyle.

How feasible is it to save a million dollars? It is highly feasible because a lot of people have already achieved this and I will show you how. How badly do you want to achieve this savings goal? Also, how much capital do you have to start with, or do you have a way to acquire any investment capital? With a solid plan, within reasonable limits, nothing is impossible.

PART I

HOW CAN YOU LIVE OFF ONE MILLION

Chapter 1 - The Elusive Million

You might be familiar with the statement "the first million is the hardest to earn", and there is some trace of truth to this. Many millionaires attest to the fact that earning your first million is the most challenging part of the journey to wealth.

This one-million challenge can be difficult for most people especially those who have nothing to begin with. But once you have managed to earn your first million, earning the subsequent millions becomes easy.

The more you understand the difficulties that go into earning your first million, the better the odds that you can easily overcome these obstacles and finally achieve this milestone.

For a start, it is crucial to understand the difference between making $1 million and owning $1 million. While earning an accumulated million can be achieved by many of us, only very few can manage to earn this amount in a single year.

Furthermore, finding a job that will allow you to earn a million dollars in one year may not always leave you really wealthy. You can easily find horror stories about lottery winners, CEOs, entertainers, and athletes who received millions only to squander their wealth away in an instant and ended up bankrupt.

There are also "millionaires" who are earning millions but also living on debt that exceeds their income. Someone could bring home $1 million in earnings but has to pay most of it for expenses. Similarly, owning a property that is worth $1 million but secured by $1.5 million in debt is not real wealth.

One of the largest obstacle to keeping $1 million in the bank is that there are not that many people who save early. Even though there are career opportunities that will allow you to earn $60,000 in excess, these are real exception. At most, newly graduates are making ends meet to repay their student loans, pay rent, and try to live the life they want. Even if you develop the strict habit of saving at least $10,000 per year, it will take more than six decades to build $1 million with no compounding interest. And by that time, inflation has eaten up much of the value of this amount and $1 million today could end up valuing as low as $ 500,000 after 60 years.

However, as we advance in age and in our careers, earning money and saving becomes a lot easier. Aside from the fact that you can usually see your income rise as you gain more experience and leverage on your expertise, you may no longer need to pay so much for the beginning expense. After a decade or so, you might have already managed to settle your student loans, and possibly you might have already found someone to share the load.

Five Reasons Why It Is Most Difficult to Earn Your First Million

Below are the top reasons why earning your first million can be the most challenging, and these are all based on how we think about wealth.

Psychological Barriers

Most of us have fears, doubts, and believe that we are incapable of earning such a big amount of money. But when we achieve something that is not usual, the worry, the fear, and the doubt will be dispelled.

Earning your next millions can be easier, because your mind is already wired for achieving this goal. Once you eliminate psychological barriers, the direct route to financial success will become more apparent.

Creative Thinking

Most people achieve their first million through creative problem solving, technological innovation, or service providing. This encourages us to continue using creative thinking solutions and strategies. Many people who have not yet earned their first million think of earning money in a linear way, which is through gainful employment. In other words, they trade their time for money.

However, real wealth is a product of creative thinking. Earning money through ideas that can solve real problems is a sure way to earn not only your first million, but also your subsequent millions. Remember, there is no limit in creative thinking, so there should be not limit on how much money you could earn in the process.

Mental Resolve

When you are working hard and smart to earn your first million, you can develop strong mental resolve. This will become one of your strongest assets to help you achieve this goal.

Experiencing success will feed your mind and spirit that will allow you to grow stronger. Using your new resolve, the momentum can continue to build up into a powerful reserve, which you can tap on as you learn how to build your wealth. Moreover, the challenge of earning your first million also involves the realization that you need dedication and time to achieve this feat.

Emotional Drive

After earning your first million, you will realize that this financial dream can become a tangible reality. You will develop the emotional motivation so you can move faster and grab every opportunity to earn your first million. The actual achievement of earning your first million will erase any doubt and you can strongly face critics and skeptics who can hinder your success.

Your enthusiasm in whatever way you think is most suitable for your circumstances will expedite your wealth acquisition. Achieving the challenge of earning $1 million will breed positive and self-affirming element that could fortify your confidence towards building your wealth. Fortunately, we are living in a society that has unlimited mechanisms for rewarding people who solve problems.

You can be as rich as you want, but it will depend on the problems that you can solve and the value you create. The naysayers and people with the poor mindset believe that being rich is only reserved for those who have privilege in the society. But once you achieve the challenge of earning your first million, you will realize that this is not a privilege but a right because anyone is free to be rich in our society.

Self-Confidence

The potential to earn will increase once you prove to yourself that you are capable of earning your first million. Surprisingly, you can feel relaxation after seeing that you have $1 million in the bank. You have managed to achieve this challenge, so you are more confident that you can do it over and over again. The confidence brought by your first million will enable you to focus on your next challenge. More often than not, we play a critical role in what is standing in the way of achieving this goal, and when you overcome yourself, your confidence raises up, and you can have the resolve that you can achieve anything.

Chapter 2 - The Millionaire Mindset

The thing that separates millionaires from average people is not luck and not even talent. Millionaires are distinct on the way they think. What enables an individual to accumulate wealth and restricts another person to a poor lifestyle usually boils down to perception and the way we organize things in our mind.

Who do you think must plan their finances? The rich or the poor? Most people would say that the poor people are in more need of financial planning compared than the rich, most importantly in the area of budgeting. However, it is the wealthy who have their own budget plan. They know where their money is coming from, and more importantly, they know where it is going.

Why is this the case? Why would wealthy people find it more important to have a financial plan compared to those who are poor? In this Chapter, I will try to show my own explanation to this concern. I am going to share my perception of the millionaire mindset. If we take a closer look, we will find that wealthy people think and see the world much differently than most people.

I personally believe that we are what we think. Below are the particular mindset that sets wealthy people apart.

Money Is Not Evil

Most people who are born poor tend to stay poor because they have a negative association with money. They believe that money is the root of all evil. That's why people who believe in this usually earn some amount of money and end up losing all of them by the end of the day. But millionaires don't believe in this nonsense. Money is just a tool invented by humankind for progress. It is completely up to us where and how we use this tool.

Time Is Not Equal to Money

Time is a finite resource, which is why it is not a good idea to trade your time for money. Rather than getting paid for their time as hired hand, millionaires devote their time in building real assets that make them even more money. Most millionaires own several businesses, which means they source their income from multiple sources.

Endless Opportunities

People who have the millionaire mindset tend to see opportunities everywhere. Every problem and every pain is an opportunity to build a service or a product. Whenever you find a space that a product or a service can fill, consider it as an opportunity to make money.

Mentorship

Finding a mentor can lead to the exponential growth of a millionaire. It is valuable to learn from others who have actually achieved earning millions. This is on a higher level of learning that what is provided via a webinar or a book. This type of learning is unique specifically to your area of interest.

Relentless Workmanship

Millionaires are naturally relentless in working towards their goals. But they also don't merely work hard. Rather, they are working smart to make sure that they can maximize their income opportunities at the shortest possible time.

Masters of the Art of Execution

Those who are trying to be rich tend to be stuck in the learning mode. Many are reading tons of books or paying for a lot of online courses to learn how to build wealth. However, they end up doing nothing. Millionaires are the opposite. They will learn the fundamentals of wealth building, then they start executing their plans. Majority of the lessons are learned through experience.

Profit is More Important than Revenue

Most millionaires put more value on profit than revenue. And if you think about it, it's not surprising at all. Ten per cent of $200,000 is only $20,000 while 50% of $40,000 is also $20,000. Hence, you should carefully choose which business you want to own. Certainly, revenue really matters. A business cannot be called a major money maker if it has a 50% profit margin but only gives you $20,000 per month.

In making more money and achieving financial independence, the wealthy develop valuable financial habits to ensure that they will not lose their money. The key to being a true millionaire is to earn $1 million, and make sure it will grow over time.

In the process of developing your own millionaire mindset, among the best financial habits that you can develop is seeking reliable financial advice before you do anything with your finances. Look for a financial advisor who also achieved the $1 million goal. He/she must also have invested personally in the endeavors that he/she recommends.

It is crucial that you be diligent before you make any form of investment. Set aside enough time to know your investment options before you even spend a dime.

More often than not, financial decisions made out of a whim turned out to be poor financial decisions. Take your time, but do respond to the opportunity without anyone pressuring you to make a decision. Most financial decisions are not urgent, and no one is compelling you to make an immediate decision. A millionaire friend of mine once told me, "Investment opportunities are like taxi cabs; there will always be another one available as long as you know how to wait. But you should not waste your time waiting and pick your ride or else you will be left behind."

There are instances that the best investments are those that you didn't place your bet at all. It is crucial that you gain a comprehensive understanding of an investment before you spend your hard-earned money. If there is one area that you don't understand then it is best not to make an investment at all.

Never Put Your Faith on Luck

Another important value in developing a millionaire mindset is getting insurance to cover the risk of losing all your investments. It is just surprising how many people have spent years saving money then lose it all just because they don't have the right insurance. While optimism is a good trait to develop, you still need to face the reality that the worst thing could happen. Be sure to always ask yourself what is the worst thing that could happen in your present situation.

Getting an insurance to protect your money is crucial because you will have a buffer account that you can use during emergencies instead of using your own money. Another advantage of being insured is that it will provide you a feeling of confidence and calmness, which allows you to think clearly and you can be more effective in any investment opportunity you take.

Protect Your Assets

As you start your journey towards wealth accumulation, you should also make certain that you protect your assets from any unnecessary lawsuits or taxes. Hire a reliable lawyer who can help you in estate planning. One option is to set up a limited partnership within the family so you can transfer your assets into the company. This way, you protect your assets from too much taxes and lawsuits. Millionaires plan so they can keep their wealth and protect it from any risk.

Beyond the Millionaire Mindset

Earning your first million and ensuring that you keep it and let it grow is a wonderful goal that you can set. However, always bear in mind that this is not the bottom line. It is the type of individual you become in terms of persistence, intelligence, character, and courage that is more important. As the outcome of becoming wealthy, you can be more satisfied and happy with yourself as well as other aspects of your life. Remember, money is just a tool, which you can use to make yourself happy as well as the people around you.

Chapter 3 - The Four Percent Rule

Let me tell you about the story of my friend Andre. After I taught him the four per cent rule, he became successful in his investments and started making his way to a million dollars.

My buddy was disciplined in withdrawing only this percentage since if he withdraws more at any given year, it may result in the principle being eroded, and reduce the actual amount they can withdraw in later years. To ensure that the one million lasts for the remainder of your life, you should already have paid off major debts such as your mortgage, otherwise you would have to pay for them with your withdrawals and this would affect how much you can live on.

Financial planners often use the 4% rule to help retirees determine the withdrawal rate from their portfolio. Life expectancy is the crucial factor in figuring out if this rate can be sustainable, because retirees who are living longer need a portfolio that can also last longer. Meanwhile, medical expenses and other living costs could also increase as you age.

The 4% rule was derived from historical data on bond and stock returns over a five-decade period from 1926 to 1976. Before the 1990s, 5 per cent was considered a safe percentage for retirees to withdraw every year. However, William Bengen, a financial advisor, performed a comprehensive research on the historical returns, with special attention on serious market crashes in the 1930s and in the 1970s. The study concluded that even during market downturns, there are no historical evidences showing that a 4 per cent withdrawal each year has exhausted the retirement portfolio in less than three decades.

However, there are certain circumstances in which the 4% rule may not be ideal for retirement. If your portfolio is composed of high-risk investment instruments over conventional index bonds and funds, you should be more conservative in withdrawing funds, specifically during the early years of your retirement. A protracted or severe market crash could erode the value of a high-risk portfolio. Moreover, the 4% rule may not work unless you are consistent in following it. Going beyond this limit to splurge on a luxury could have serious consequences because the principal from which the interest is compounded will be decreased.

For example, say that you have $500,000 in your retirement fund and the existing inflation rate is 3%. In this case, you can withdraw 4% of your retirement fund plus an added 3% to cover the inflation. IN following the 4% rule, your withdrawals in the first three years will look like this:

       Year 1 - $20,000 (4% of $500,000)
       Year 2 - $20,600 ($20,000 plus 3% or $600)

Year 3 - $21,218 ($20,600 plus 3% or $618)

Sticking to a fixed percentage of withdrawal has its own advantages. First, it will allow you to keep a base withdrawal at a specific level from the First Year of retirement. In putting a cap on your withdrawal, you will not be tempted to spend all your money at once, and you can plan ahead your expenses for the next years to come.

There are also different investments with a higher return rate beyond 4% that you will all learn in this book so you can add more revenue for your portfolio even if you withdraw. When you receive added interest payments, dividends or earnings that is not from your investment portfolio, you can consider this as extra money, which you can include in your 4% on top of the inflation rate.

Sticking to a withdrawal limit will help you become more discipline in your expenditures as well as carry on the risk of inflation. This will help you make sure that your $1 million will not be depleted soon.

Earning a million can be achieved in as short as one year. However, it may take several years before you can find the right investment instrument and determine the right withdrawal strategy that is most suitable for your needs. Even the 4% rule has its own disadvantages.

Primarily, with people now living longer than expected, there is a high chance that a 4% withdrawal could be even higher. That is why some planners are now recommending 2 to 3% annual withdrawal rate, which can match our increasing life expectancy.

If your portfolio is composed of bonds, stocks, and other investment instruments, you can have a chance to maximize your revenue to cover your needs towards retirement.

Also take note that the 4% rule is not a hard and fast rule, since it does not project annual adjustments for inflation, which can have an impact to your investment returns. In the United States, the Federal Reserve is working on a 2% inflation rate. If your portfolio earns negative yearly returns, it could mean a 4% withdrawal could exhaust your fund faster than you need to. This will make it hard to recover from losses if you don't have a regular income.

Meanwhile, the market may outperform any expectation, which could boost the value of your retirement fund. In this case, a 4% withdrawal rate may not be sufficient. If the economic conditions are good, you may end up with more funds than you need. Hence, you can enjoy a higher withdrawal rate and improve your lifestyle.

Withdrawing just 4% could be too much if your funds are not enough to cover the lifestyle you want to live. Take note that you can always adjust your withdrawal rate if you only have less than a decade before you retire. Below are some things that you should keep in mind:

- <u>Be aggressive in your savings</u>

    Setting aside money for your life goals such as your first home, sending your kids to college, emergency fund or a major purchase may not be easy. Retirement should not be left out. It is best to start your retirement fund as early as possible and start saving as much as you can.

- <u>Create multiple income streams</u>

    It is crucial to have multiple income streams. Depending solely on one income can put a lot of strain on your finance. And in retirement fund, you should also have different sources of income such as rental business or stocks. You might be able to reduce your portfolio withdrawal rate and depend less on your savings if you have enough fund to cover some basic expenses such as food, housing, medicine, and bills.

- <u>Have a budget and stick to it</u>

    Let's say you managed to earn $1 million in one year, but you don't have a budget plan, and you continued splurging your money. This will result in your wealth depleting in no time at all. As early as today, you can start working on your budget, keep track of your cash flow, and look for creative ways to cut back on your expenses in order to save money as much as you can.

You can follow the 4% rule as a fixed withdrawal rate, which will allow you for generous withdrawals, allow you to keep your money and keep up with inflation rates. By earning a million dollar in one year and having a plan to make sure it doesn't go away, you can start paving the way towards wealth and financial freedom.

The 7% Rule

Another approach to living off one million is to adjust your withdrawals to the returns you are getting in a particular year. For instance, if you are enjoying a 7% return, you can withdraw that much from your nest egg or you can withdraw a smaller percentage and add the remainder to your investment capital to increase the base and boost the returns you get in future years.

To successfully do this, you have to create a portfolio of fixed income investments with consistent annual returns. But the problem with these investments is that since the returns don't greatly increase over time, there is a risk that your returns will be eroded by inflation, which historically average around 3% a year. As you get older, your health expenses may also increase since you may need to spend more on health care and prescription medications.

Basically, 4% is considered safe withdrawal, while 7% is regarded as an optimal withdrawal. It is crucial to determine which withdrawal rate is suitable for you depending on your portfolio. There are instances that even the 4% can be too high for those that are focused on identifying sustainable withdrawal rate, which could not deplete the portfolio over a 30-year period.

But take note that this doesn't necessarily forbid using the 4% or higher withdrawal rate. You may still select a withdrawal rate that is higher than this to downplay the possible effect of depleting your investment portfolio.

In addition, rather than focusing on the conventional goal of concerning only about employing lower rate as a failure buffer, financial advisors recommend seeking balance between two major choices:
- Enjoying retirement while you are still healthy
- Avoiding the depletion of portfolio and instead depend on non-portfolio income sources in retirement

In general, if you are less flexible with your expenditures and you are more averse in longevity risk, you may want to smooth out spending during retirement. It is ideal not to increase your spending if the market is performing well, and instead focus on maintaining the stability of your spending if you end up living longer as expected.

Thus, the best way to live off one million is to use it to create income. There are a variety of ways you can do this.

- Purchase a rental property. You can buy rental properties for an average $100,000 each and earn around $100,000 in annual rental income. Of course, you would have to invest some money in repairs and maintenance expenses, but you could take out a loan on the properties and pay it off using the rental income.
- Invest in growth stocks. These are stocks issued by companies with high growth prospects and are expected to generate returns at a higher rate than the market average. Thus, the investor would enjoy high capital gains when they decide to sell their shares.
- Invest in dividend-paying stocks. These stocks will not only provide you with some capital gains but also give you some income that you can use for living expenses or reinvest in more stock or other assets.

In addition, to safeguard your capital, you should also place your money in some safer assets, such as gold, which holds its value over the long-term, and US Treasury securities, which are backed by the US dollar.

Now that you have saved one million dollars, there are two ways that you can live off it – by drawing from it at a given rate or by investing it to generate income.

PART II

MAKING ONE MILLION IN ONE YEAR

Chapter 4 - Real Estate

What are your possibilities for making a million dollars in one year? In this section, we will discuss the best options available that made a lot of people I know truly wealthy.

There are basically two ways you can make money from real estate, either through rental income or by flipping properties. Flipping involves buying a house, doing the necessary repairs or refurbishments to the property, and then reselling it at a higher price. Although this will take time and a huge initial investment, you can easily make a million dollars if you strike the right deals.

Making a Profit from Rental Property

There is a lot of work involved in sorting out a property for rental income from your first decision to invest in rental property to actually purchasing your property investment. This task could be overwhelming for beginners, as becoming a landlord can be a challenging career, and the risk is also high. That is why you need to minimize your risk and maximize your returns to make this project a worthwhile investment.

While you can hire a real estate agent to help you complete your rental property, you must begin looking for investments on your own. Working too early with an agent may bring excessive pressure to purchase a property before you even complete your search for properties that are suitable for you. It is important that you receive an objective approach for all properties that you are considering within your investment range.

Your range of investment can be restricted depending on your preference to manage the property or hire a property manager. If you want to become an active landlord, it is ideal to find a property that is nearby your residence. If you want to hire a property manager, work on the numbers if you can afford to pay his or her salary.

Below are the top things that you must consider when you are looking for a property for rental income.

Quality of Neighborhood

It is crucial to make sure that you buy a property in a decent neighborhood, because this will affect the types of tenants that you like and how often you may experience vacancies. For instance, if you get a property in a neighborhood that is just blocks away from a university, then there is a high chance that your tenants are primarily composed of university students and that you can face regular vacancies.

Rental Income

Remember, rental income will become the bread and butter of your real estate investment. Hence, you must be aware of the average rent in your area. If the rent is not enough to pay for your overhead expenses inclusive of mortgage payment and taxes, then you need to keep looking. Make certain that you do your due diligence about the area so you can measure where the area is headed in the next five years. You can still go bankrupt if you need to make expensive repairs and improvements to the house, and if the property taxes in the area are higher than you expected they would be.

Property Taxes

Take note that property taxes vary from one state to another, and in this form of investment, you need to make sure that you are familiar with this important payable. Also bear in mind that high property taxes is just normal in decent neighborhood, which is ideal if you are looking for long-term tenants. You can consult the local property assessment office, or you could talk to current homeowners in the community.

Crime Index

No one likes to live in an area where the crime index is quite high. Make certain that you visit the police for accurate crime index for different neighborhoods. Don't rely on the current homeowner because he has interest in selling the property for a higher price. Be sure to know the incidence of petty crimes, vandalism, and recent growth or decrease. You should also know the police visibility in the neighborhood.

Job Market

Areas with increasing job opportunities have the higher tendency to entice more people, so you can expect high surge of tenants. You can visit the local library or go directly to a local office of the Bureau of Labor Statistics to figure out the local job rate. If there is an announcement from a large company building offices in an area, more workers will move near the area. But this may also cause the prices to go up or down depending on the company that is moving in.

Schools

Buying a rental property near schools is ideal if you want to attract people with children and with jobs. But be sure to check the quality of the school as this could have an impact on the value of your investment. If the school has a bad reputation, the price could reflect the value of the property. While you might be concerned about your regular income, the overall property value is also crucial if you are planning to sell it in the future.

Vacancies and Listings

A neighborhood may not be ideal for a rental property if there is an unusual high number of listings as this is often an indicator of a seasonal cycle. Be sure to check this before you buy a property. You must also figure out if you could cover for any seasonal vacancies. Vacancy rates will also provide you an idea of how you can effectively entice tenants. Higher vacancy rates could push landlords to cut down on rent to avoid vacancies. Lower vacancy rates also allow landlords to increase rent.

Future Development and Building Permits

You can visit the local planning office to gather information on the future developments that are in placed in the neighborhood. It can be an ideal growth community if there are several malls, business parks, or condos for construction. But be sure to watch out for new developments, which could damage the price of surrounding properties. For example, new condos or housing projects can increase the competition in the area.

Natural Disasters

Another expense that you need to consider is insurance. You need to include this in your overhead expenses. Hence, be sure that you are aware of how much you need to cover. If the area is prone to floods, hurricane or earthquake, make certain that you work on the insurance premium and find out if you can still make a profit if you choose the property.

Basically, the ideal investment property for starters is a condominium unit or a single-family residential home. While condos may have higher price tag, it can mean lower maintenance, as the condo developer typically has association that can help in external repairs. As condos are not really independent residential units, they usually carry lower rental rates and has slower appreciation rate compared to single-family homes.

Single-family residences can easily entice long-term tenants. In general, a family or a couple are ideal renters because they are more financially stable, can regularly pay the rent, and don't easily move around. As an investor in rental property, you might need to look for a property and an area, which can entice this type of tenants.

If you have already chosen a specific neighborhood, you should look for a property, which has the best potential for appreciation as well as a good projected cash flow. Be sure to check out properties that carry higher price tag alongside those that are within your capital.

Take note that real property usually sell below the listing price.

Keep track of the listing prices of other units, and make certain that you also ask the final selling price so you have an idea of the property's market value. For potential appreciation, you can look for a property, which requires minimal renovation, and can entice tenants who are willing to pay higher rent. This can be also for your advantage, as you can easily increase the property's value if you want to sell this after several years.

When it comes to cash flow, you may need to work on a smart guess. You have to take the average rental in the area then deduct your projected monthly mortgage payments, insurance cost (divide by 12 months), property taxes (also divide by 12 months), and standby funds for repairs and maintenance. Always have a buffer fund and never underestimate the cost of maintenance. When all these numbers come out with a substantial net profit, then you can start working on with your real estate agent so you can submit an offer.

Real Estate Appreciation

A major source of money from real estate is through appreciation, which refers to the increase of value of the property. You can achieve this in various ways various forms of real estate. But take note that you can only realize this profit if you refinance the property or sell it.

If you choose to invest in undeveloped lands, you can also make money when it appreciates. As your area becomes more progressive, the surrounding lands can become more valuable because the potential to be purchased by developers become higher. Real estate developers can also build structures that further increase this value.

Raw land can also appreciate in value if there are valuable minerals or materials discovered as long as you own the rights of the property. One example of this is when the land has been discovered to have mineral deposits or oil.

In looking at residential properties, location is also the major factor to consider. As your area becomes more developed, the addition of playgrounds, shopping centers, schools, and roads, can increase the value of the property. Certainly, this system can also work against you if the value of the homes plummet because of bad neighborhood.

Improving the residential property can also affect property appreciation, and fortunately you can control this factor. Redesigning the kitchen, adding a pool, installing centralized temperature control can increase the value of the property. This is usually done in house flipping as you can easily increase the value of the home in a short period of time.

You should also take note that property appreciation is also affected by inflation. A 5%

dollar inflation means that your money can only buy around 95% of the same property the next year.

For example, if a property was worth $50,000 in 1972, and it was never developed, and sat idle, the value of the land will be higher today. Because of inflation, the price of the property could be $ 250,000 today, assuming that $50,000 was a fair market value.

House Flipping

Basically, you need a set of special skills if you want to go into house flipping. Project management is a basic skill that you should master alongside negotiating and comprehensive understanding of the real estate market. Being savvy in your finances and having great work ethics can also help a lot.

Searching for the Right Area for House Flipping

An important step to a profitable house flipping is having a comprehensive knowledge of the market that you like to work in. Unfortunately, this is also the step, which many beginner house flippers usually ignore. If you want to be profitable in house flipping, then you must know the market.

First, you should be aware of how much are home selling for. To determine great deals, which have the possibility to be resold or renovated, you must be aware of the average price homes are selling for in the market. You should also be able to break this down by the home types sold. For instance, two bedroom apartments may be affordable in the area, but four-bedroom mansions also carry a premium price tag.

Seller's Market vs. Buyer's Market

One good measure of how fast homes are selling in an area is by getting the months supply, which is basically the number of months it may take in order to sell the homes presently on the market in a certain neighborhood.

To determine the months supply in an area, you must first figure out how many houses are presently on the market and the number of houses sold every month. You may ask a real estate agent to do this for you. After getting this data, you just need to divide the number of houses presently on the market against the number of houses sold every month. For instance, if there are 30 homes on the market and there are 6 houses that can be sold every month, there are six months of supply in that area.

It is considered a seller's market if the number is lower than six months, and a buyer's market if the number is more than six month. You can save a lot of money if you know the difference between the two.

Take note that because you will be on the sell side and the buy side within the same year, you might probably want to try and concentrate on neighborhoods with less than 6 months of supply. There is a possibility that your flipped house may stay in the market beyond your financial capacity.

Searching for Local Real Estate Market Trends

When you have a solid grasp on the pricing in your local market, you must dig down a bit deeper then figure out where the prices could go by next year and then the succeeding year. You must read local press, blogs, and local social media groups to find the local market trends.

For instance, probably there is a new shopping district to be constructed in an area which will attract hundreds of employees. This could mean increase of rental prices. There can also be a change in the demographic in the area that will result to increase prices. It will help you identify deals worth pursuing if you know the market in the neighborhood and the surrounding areas.

It can be a Challenge to Flip Houses in a Low Income Neighborhood

In the onset, your calculations may not what it seems. It could show a strong market with less than six months of inventory. But this could forego the shadow inventory, which could exist in the neighborhood. There could also be a high number of houses owned by lenders or foreclosed homes in the community. If possible, try getting the number of foreclosed properties, as passing this on may not provide you a true picture of how many homes are available to buy.

Also, you must take note that a high number of foreclosure in an area can be an indicator that the neighborhood is on a decline. Crime can be another concern in renovating as well as selling a home in a bad neighborhood. For example, some contractors are not confident in leaving expensive materials and equipment on the property, and may even be not willing to work there. In selling, you may find it difficult to find more interested and decent buyers.

Try to Look for Houses to Flip on More Decent Neighborhoods

While it can be a bit harder to look for good deals and the competition could be high, working in more decent neighborhoods could save you a lot of disappointment and stress.

The best market for house flipping are those with increasing populations, strong local investment, and diverse economies. And in selecting a neighborhood in any market, you must concentrate on those with great job opportunities, easy access for transportation, and decent schools.

How to Look for Houses to Flip

While there's no guaranteed way to look for houses to fix and flip, advertising, driving through your target area, and referrals are all good methods to look for homes that you can fix and flip.

A good way to search for homes to flip is to walk, bike, or drive through an area that you want to work in. Try to spot homes that are poorly kept or looks vacant. If you call the owner, you may learn that they are ready to move or behind their mortgage payments.

Another method to find house flipping deals is by networking with other real estate brokers. But it will help a lot if you first build an outstanding reputation in the industry. Real estate professionals such as contractors and brokers may not have the connections, resources, or the time to flip home at a profit.

Rather, they could just refer a list on someone they trust in exchange of a minimal finder's fee.

Take a Closer Look at the House for Flipping

After getting a list of homes that can be flipped, you should next set an appointment with the owner of the house. It is ideal to bring along your contractor. This is to readily assess the need for renovation and possible expenses right along.

You must also figure out the After Repair Value or ARV of the home. To work on this number, you must go back to your listing and look for homes that were recently sold, which are similar in condition and size when you are done with the planned repairs.

You should not also forget the 70% rule. Take note that the objective of any house flipping is to sell the home for a price that is not only better than your agreed price with the old house owner but also more than the buying price on top of the repair costs, contractor costs, carrying fees, and other expenses.

To do this, profitable house flippers follow the 70% rule. In general, you must try to pay only 70 per cent of the ARV less than the cost of repairs.

For example, if a house that you want to flip has an ARV of $500,000 and your contractor requires $50,000 for the whole repair. The first thing that you need to do is to get the 70 per cent of the ARV, which is $350,000. The next step is to subtract the cost of renovation that will leave you with $300,000. Hence, to make sure that you can obtain a reasonable revenue on this project, the most that you can offer for the house is $300,000.

If you take a loan of $300,000 at 10% interest, below are the possible cost that you need to consider. Take note that these numbers are generous estimates.
- Amount you pay for the house to flip - $ 300,000
- Repair costs - $50,000
- Loan origination fee - $ 3000 to $ 5000
- Realtor's commission - $0 to $30,000
- Buying costs - 0 to 3% of the sales price
- Selling costs - 0 to 3% of the sales price

In addition, you should also consider the number of months it will take you to sell the home. If it takes four months, then you have to pay the cost of owning the home for four months. These are known as carrying costs or holding expenses.

Types of Repairs That Can Increase House Prices

Even though homes with great ventilation and hardwood floors are certainly attractive to potential buyers, it is ideal not to focus too much on the present aesthetics of the home when you first visit it. Rather, you must spot on possible repairs. A mansion that requires

$35,000 electrical and plumbing work will heavily cost you and will definitely make you less money compared to a duplex that will only need new tiles and new windows.

In general, the kitchen is considered as the most significant room in a home, so it is not surprising that renovating your kitchen could translate to higher profit for you. It may take around $20,000 to renovate a kitchen, but the average profit on investment for this is around 80 %. However, the real advantage of a kitchen renovation is in its ability to entice more people to buy the home. The property can be sold faster if the kitchen is great. Just be sure that the kitchen is on par with the rest of the houses in the market.

Replacement windows can also increase the overall selling price of your flipped home. On average, a vinyl window can provide you as much as 78 per cent of the initial price. Wooden windows are also great, which can provide you at least 79 to 80% ROI. A front door replacement can also increase your profit to as much as 102% of your initial investment.

Below are some more repairs that can help you get more revenue from flipping houses:
- Tilework - Replacing old kitchen and bathroom tiles is a cost-effective and easy improvement that can substantially improve the aesthetics of the house.
- Renovating Kitchens and Bathrooms - Aside from doing the tilework, getting a replacement for bath fixtures as well as

- getting new kitchen appliances can also add more revenue to your bottom line.
- Opening enclosed dining rooms or kitchens - Many house buyers today are looking for homes that are open. It makes the house bigger and can bring more light into darker areas.
- Adding a bedroom - Even though this could take more work and will probably require additional permits, adding another bedroom to a one-bedroom house can provide you large returns.
- Adding a basement - While you may not be allowed to call a basement as a bedroom, potential buyers are still enticed by added space that they could use as guest room or home office.

Once you have finally found the home that you can flip, the next step is to complete your due diligence and look for more repairs that can increase the home value. You should always be present during home inspection, but getting the services of a professional house inspector can help a lot.

Once you find the right property to flip, you will usually have to pay a down payment in cash (which can be around 25% of the selling price) plus closing costs and then pay for repairs out of pocket. Other costs you will have to shoulder include homeowner's insurance, utilities such as water and electricity and maintenance costs.

If you don't have the capital needed to front these flipping costs, you will either have to take out a loan to cover them or find an investor willing to provide you with working capital. Of course, in the latter case, your potential profit is reduced since you will have to provide the investor with a certain amount of the selling price of the house as his return. If you are having trouble getting financing from the usual sources, there are hard money lenders that specialize in providing loans for flipping houses, but they charge higher rates than traditional lenders, have a shorter repayment period and typically use the property as collateral. On the other hand, they are easier to acquire than bank loans and, since the loans come from private lenders, you may be able to negotiate more flexible repayment terms.

Another problem you will face when trying to make a million dollars from flipping houses is that you will have to make many deals before you reach this profit goal. You will not earn a lot from a single flipping transaction, although the amount of your profit will vary depending on the value of the property and the neighborhood in which it is located. In addition, it takes time to complete repairs and then find a buyer for the property once you've refurbished it. Until then, your money is tied up in the property and you cannot use it for other purposes.

Paying for House Flipping

It can be a challenge to determine how you can pay for homes that you are interested in flipping. Of course, there are only few lenders who are willing to bet on homes in poor condition, or if you can't provide proof that you have high net worth and you have steady income. Fortunately, there are special lenders who offer their services for house flippers.

Traditional Bank Loans

Traditional bank loans are ideal for experienced house flippers. Most banks are offering traditional mortgage loan. Again, because most banks are not interested in investing in houses that are in poor condition, this could be a challenge for amateur house flippers. This can be trickier if you don't have significant assets that you can place as collateral.

Hard Money Lenders

Hard money lenders are ideal for beginners or those with bad credit. These lenders are basically composed of investors who are willing to lend cash to house flippers. The primary reason why house flippers prefer hard money lenders is that these lenders know the industry well and they also care about the ARV of the home than your financial record or your experience. Hard money lenders are also great financiers for purchasing foreclosed homes, regardless if you want to turn the property into rental or for house flipping. Most hard money lenders are offering 12-month loans with interest rate beginning between 6% and 7%. The approval can be as short as two weeks.

Private Cash Lenders

Private cash lenders are ideal for beginners in the house flipping world or if you have bad credit. These lenders are similar to hard money lenders, but the main difference is that they are basically made of smaller investors, and in some cases just one person. Because there are numerous private money lenders, it is ideal to obtain a referral from more experienced house flippers.

House Flipping Crowdfunding Loans

Crowdfunding a home for flipping is ideal for experienced house flippers who are in need of money fast. This option is composed of large pool of lenders, so you can get the cash you need immediately for as short as 2 to 3 days. This option is also ideal if you have already finished house flipping projects for quite some time.

Chapter 5 - Stock Market

You can make a million dollars in the stock market, but you will need to do a lot of homework before you make your first investment. Investing is an inherently risky activity and it is very possible that your investment can be wiped out by a few bad decisions. So you have to study the market to determine the best place to put your money.

The equities market have yielded long-term gains that are larger than those of any other types of asset class. From 1926, big stocks have provided an average of 10% per annum. It is also interesting to take note that these stocks did not lose any ground during any period of two decades or longer. These features make stocks more enticing for long-term savings instead of bonds that may only yield around 5.6% average yearly gains. The return potential of stocks can provide you the best chance to be protected from inflation in the long-term. This is why stocks are important component of a retirement portfolio that will allow you to earn a million dollars in one year.

One of the quickest ways to make money is to find stocks whose prices are on an upswing. You simply buy the stock when the price starts to rise and then sell your shares once the price hits a certain level. The success of this strategy depends on your finding "hot" stocks whose values are appreciating quickly, and then determining the best time to sell where you can maximize your profit while minimizing your risk.

Another strategy that lets you make a lot of money from the stock market is to short sell. This method is effective during bear markets when prices are going down. Of course, this strategy carries a lot of risk and you can easily lose your capital but if you make wise decisions, you can earn high returns.

If you are willing to invest over a longer period, you can buy stocks from promising companies such as technology startups that might suddenly become very valuable if they take off and become very profitable.

If your capital is limited, you can increase your investing power by availing of leverage. Leverage essentially means that you are buying stocks using borrowed capital. To use leverage you will only need to have a relatively small amount in your trading account and the amount you can trade will be magnified depending on how much leverage your broker will provide. Leverage is expressed as a ratio, i.e. 1:20, meaning that for every $1 in your account, you can trade $20. Thus, if you have $1,000 in your trading account, you can control up to $20,000 worth of stocks.

In order to successfully reach your goal, you have to make a trading plan. This plan will define what your strategy will be, how much you will risk per trade, how much leverage you will use, and other aspects of your trading activity. It is important that you not only create a trading plan, but also have the discipline to stick to it.

You also need to learn how to analyze the markets to identify which stocks to invest in. This means doing a lot of reading to find out which companies are hot right now as well as which may be hot in the future. There are a wide variety of online resources that you can access to do this research.

How Long It Will Take to Earn $1 Million in the Stock Market

Earning a million dollars in the stock market will greatly depend on how much you start with, how much and how often you can add to your investment, and how much you could earn over time.

For instance, if you have $100,000 and invest it into equities, in less than 16 years, this investment can turn into a million dollars. Take note that this is based in the US exchange with a yearly return of at least 10 % over the long term on top of the dividends. If you invest $20,000 every year into a tax-deferred fund, you may need around 12 years before you can enjoy $1 million profit.

Current Bullish Market in the US

At present, the US market is into a bullish trend, and since 2009 the stock prices have increased into three-fold. Because high share price make purchasing stocks more expensive, it can result to lower returns. Some stock analysts believe that over the next decade, stocks could provide an average between 6.5 to 7 per cent, in which case investing $20,000 per year will take around 15 years to reach a million dollars.

You can take advantage of market declines by buying stocks at a lower price, which in the long-term can provide you sizeable returns. The higher the share price drops, the more chances you can take advantage in purchasing equities at a discount.

The best way to do this to improve your gains and obtain higher returns is known as buying in dips. In this strategy, if the stock market plummets 10 per cent, you can take advantage of the drop by purchasing more stocks. Then you can purchase more if the market plummets another 10%.

A large blunder that most people make is that they withdraw their investment once it drops, when instead, this is the time that they should buy more. Just stick to your strategy, be disciplined through the market fluctuations and in time you can earn a million dollars.

It will take substantial capital to earn $1 million in one year through stock investment. Hence, you can use this income stream as part of your overall revenue plan.

Earning Money in the Stock Market

There are two main ways that you can earn money in the stock market. First, you can earn profit if the stocks you purchase appreciate in value. This can happen if people who like to purchase the stock decides that a share is valued higher compared to the price that you have paid for it. For instance, shareholders may see it this way if the company issuing the stock has improved earnings in the past year.

If you hold into a stock, which has appreciated in value, you can have what is known as unrealized profits. You can only lock in your gains only if you sell the stock. Because the prices of stock fluctuate consistently during open market, there is no certain way to possibly know the price until the moment you sell the shares.

Another way to earn money from the stock market is through dividend, which refers to the payout that the companies are paying the shareholders.

Some companies that are part of the stock market pays their shareholders depending on the earnings of the company. Often released every three months, dividends can provide you a regular return regardless of what can happen in the price of the stock.

More often than not, well-established companies pay dividends. Take note that dividends are not guaranteed, so any company may choose to pay their shareholders at any time. You may choose to withdraw your dividends, but it is ideal to keep reinvesting the dividends instead of spending them. The fastest way to do this is through a reinvestment scheme that makes the reinvestment automatic.

Risks in the Stock Market

In general, stocks carry more risk of losing your investment compared to cash or bond. Since the Second World War, the US stock exchange has experienced a total of six market declines or bearish market, which refers to a 20% fall in the S&P 500 value. Hence, it is not ideal to invest all your money in stocks if you need the money for the next three to five years.

How to Purchase Stocks

The easiest way to buy a stock is through stock brokers, who gets paid to trade stocks and other forms of financial securities in your behalf. Tale note that this is quite different than providing investment advice, even though some stock brokers are also professional financial advisers. Take note that there are two types of stock brokers: discount and full-service.

Full-service stock brokers are allowed to provide investment advice. You can also ask a full-service broker to manage your investment portfolio. For instance, your broker may ask between 1 per cent and

1.5 per cent of the value of your stocks. Hence, if you want to purchase $10,000 worth of stocks with 1 per cent broker fee, you need to pay $100 for this specific transaction. There are also full-service stock brokers who are charging flat fees instead of percentage.

On the other hand, discount brokers specialize in completing the transactions in your behalf for a certain price. For example, some online brokers are offering stock trades for as low as $15. Under this category, there are share brokers who charge a specific fee for every trade. Share brokers usually charge less for every share for bigger stock trades.

Regardless of what type of broker you choose, you must always set aside time to read and understand the terms and conditions and always ask for the brokerage fees. For instance, there are instances that there are special rules for trades that are lower such as the need to make specific number of trades every month or keep a minimum balance.

Various Types of Stocks

There are different types of stocks that you can choose, so it is possible that you can place stocks in various categories such as sector, style, and size. Viewing stocks this way can help you in diversifying your stock investment. Moreover, you can also select different stocks, which are different from each other in a way that they will not affect each other.

By Sector - A popular data provider, Standard & Poor's, categorize stocks into 10 different sectors and several industries. In general, various sectors can be influenced by different factors at a given period of time. Hence, some may do well than the others depending on their sector.

By Style - Basically, there are two primary forms of stocks according to style. First, a growth stock is released by a company, which is expanding at a faster than normal rate. It is ideal to invest in a growth stock early on so you have more chances for appreciation. But take note that the risk is bigger for stocks with higher potential. Growth stocks can move faster when the market conditions are good, but they could also tank during downturn.

On the other hand, a value stock has the tendency to be more stable, with strong market fundamentals. Basically, you can trade this at a lesser profit margin compared to the overall market. Some investors in the value stocks often think that the underlying business is still good and that the actual value of the stock is not yet visible in the market.

By Size - Market capitalization defines the size of a company. It also refers to the present share price multiplied by the total number of outstanding shares. This is how much investors are thinking of the whole value of the company. Companies could be categorized as large-cap, mid-cap, or small-cap. In general, large cap companies have the tendency to experience stabilized stock prices compared to small caps, so they carry less risk. However, small caps in turn provide the best potential for growth.

Stocks and Taxes

Taxation is an important factor to consider when you are into stock investment. It is ideal to place as much investment as you could into a tax-sheltered account if you are working on your retirement fund. One example of this is your 401(k). The investment into these accounts are exempted from taxation until you reach your retirement age. Hence, you can enjoy more money when you need it for your nest egg.

If you want to invest in stocks that are not under these tax-sheltered accounts, you can still do some legal ways to make sure that your taxes are at minimum. First, if the stock you buy are paying dividends, take note that these are taxed at a basic of 15% per year.

Further, if you are putting your stocks in the market for selling, then you need to pay 15% of any profits that you have made over time that you held the stock. These are referred to as capital gains, and the tax is known as capital gains tax. However, if you managed to hold a stock for less than one year before you sell it, you only need to pay your regular income tax rate on the gain, which is a rate that is typically higher compared to capital gains tax.

Important Rules to Follow in Stock Investing

The possibility of earning a lot of money has attracted a lot of investors to enter the stock markets. But making money in this financial instrument is not a walk in the park. This does not only require discipline or technical know-how, but also a lot of learning and financial judgement.

This is on top of the reality that the stock market is a highly volatile market, which can make or break your investment. Even those who are into the stock market are not always sure whether to hold, invest more, or sell their shares.

While there is no guaranteed formula to become successful in the stock market, there are timeless rules that if you follow could increase your chances in getting high profits. Check out these stock investing rules below:

1. <u>Devise a stock investment plan and follow it</u>

    Before buying any shares, you should fully understand what you are investing for. This will affect your target profit, risk appetite, time horizon, as well as the types of stocks that you should buy for your portfolio.

2. <u>Understand the stock market fundamentals before investing</u>

    It is crucial to understand the overall gist of the stock market first before you invest. The stock market is a wonderful financial system, which can make you wealthy if you know how to play the game. You will surely be disappointed if you lose your investments and you don't even know the reason why. Be sure to stick to what you know at the moment, and always ask for a mentor if you need help.

3. <u>The stock market has the tendency to correct itself</u>

In common parlance, this means that the fluctuations in the stock market is not permanent. Whether it is an upward or a downward trend, the market always correct itself for long-term levels of valuation. As an investor, you must have a plan and follow it. Never be hauled by the smaller turmoil and squawks in the market.

4. <u>Excesses are always temporary because there are never new eras</u>

   Even the most experienced investors still have the tendency to believe that if things are in their favor, the revenue could be endless, so they take their guard down. This is not the ideal strategy in the stock market. As the number one rule in this list, the stock market corrects itself. You should regard revenue as revenue while they are available, or they will be lost.

5. <u>Overcorrection can happen during extreme fluctuations</u>

   Similar to a motorcycle driven by a beginner, overcorrection can happen if the market is overshooting. Most investors would give way to fear over greed. Experienced investors are usually anxious about this and they usually possess the discipline and technical skills to take calculated steps to protect their investments.

6. Diversify

It will help a lot if you diversify your stock market portfolio with different investments from stocks of different size, style, and sector. This will ensure that your whole investment will not go down the drain if something happens that could impact one industry for instance. Try to diversify to at least 12 to 15 stocks, which is an ideal number to deal with measuring the performance, news flow, and costs. Also diversify your whole investment portfolio by also including funds, bonds, and stocks.

7. The Stock Market is Not a Popularity Game

Most players in the stock market do not fully understand the equities instrument, so they usually behave against the ideal strategy in this investment. In order to gain the best long-term revenue, there is a need to eventually sell the shares that people are buying, then purchase the stocks that are being ignored. But make sure that the shares have the right valuation, and they have the right growth potential. It takes a skilled stocks market investor to ascertain the risks and make sure that quality checks are met.

8. Reinvest Your Dividends

    In building your portfolio, it is ideal to concentrate on shares with robust competitive benefit and a great reason why they customers should continue patronizing their products and services. This will provide the pricing capacity, which empowers companies to come up with the cash and pay the dividends, which can provide you savings over time. There are also several funds that are dedicated to these companies.

9. Focus On the Value of the Company Not on the Share Price

    Be sure to prioritize the value of the company over the current price of its share. If you know that a company has outstanding reputation in the industry, it offers high-quality products and services, and managed by reputable individuals, then the company will have higher tendency to do well over time. Be sure to use your judgment to determine if the company has good value. Simple metrics to estimate the growth of the company as well as assess the risk and quality will help you decide if a valuation is low, average, or high.

10. Cash Flow is King

Take note that cash flow is based on fact, while profit can be based on opinion. Some companies may try to pump up their reported profits, but they cannot lie when it comes to cash flow. It is ideal to concentrate your due diligence on how the company is generating cash instead of its profits.

How to Choose Stocks

One challenge in stock investing is choosing stocks to buy. With thousands of stocks available in the market, it can be overwhelming especially for beginners. It can be impossible to go through every income statement and balance sheet of each company in the stock market to find those who have good net margins and favorable net debt position.

Moreover, selecting an investment that is strictly based on the criteria of a screener is vulnerable to errors and do not always provide a whole picture of a company.

Revisit Your Goals

Revisiting the purpose of your portfolio is the first step in choosing a stock from hundreds of choices available. You will surely have a different investment criteria if you are focusing on capital appreciation, capital preservation, or income. If you want your capital to appreciate, you should look for companies with wide range of market caps and different life cycle phases. Meanwhile, those who have lower risk tolerance are mainly focused on capital preservation and they have the tendency to invest in large corporations that are considered blue chips. Investors who are income oriented will normally concentrate on low-growth companies in sectors and utilities like utilities, while other alternatives like partnerships and REITs are also accessible.

Remember that diversification is a good strategy in stock investing. Hence, regardless of which investor you are, you can use a mixture of these strategies. But deciding which type of investor you are is one of the easiest part. Determining the specific stock to choose can be more complex. Even though there is no guaranteed way on how you can choose stocks, a fundamental strategy can help you filter down your search before you can begin analyzing the company financials.

Be Updated with the Current Trends

To become an informed investor, it is crucial that you are updated with the latest events in the markets and read insights from expert investors. You may read online financial news from reliable websites, magazines, and even blogs so you are updated every day. There are instances that a blog post or a news article can build the foundation of your underlying investment decision.

For instance, learning about a significant company acquisition could trigger further due diligence into the company fundamentals that can drive a certain industry or sector. The World Wide Web offers a considerable level of comfort where any significant event can be analyzed via different perspectives by various investment experts.

There are instances that the fundamental thesis could be as plain as there is a present movement away from an emerging market that is causing a higher number of people who consider themselves as middle class. And so, there can be a spike in demand for a product. If you take this thesis in a higher level, you can deduce that with a surge in the demand, the producers of this specific product might become more prosperous in the next years to come.

This form of basic analysis builds the basis of the general platform behind your stock investment that will justify buying any share in a certain industry. A crucial research need is to determine the theories and assumptions of the basic argument. If the supply A is unlimited, an increase in demand push could likely have minimal impact on companies in the business of producing product A.

When you are already convinced and comfortable of the fundamental argument after you do this type of qualitative search, investor reports and press releases are good sources for continuous analysis.

Looking for Companies to Buy

The next phase in choosing stocks to buy involves searching for the companies that you might be interested depending on your established goals. There are three basic methods on how you can do this:

First, you can look for ETFs that can monitor the performance of an industry and check your holdings. This could be as easy as like searching for a product online. Take note that the official page for a company ETF can be disclosed either on top holdings or all of the fund.

Second, you can also utilize a stock screener to make it easier for you to filter out the stocks depending on a certain criteria like industry and sector. Stock screeners usually use added features like managing companies according to market cap, yield dividend, and other valuable investment metrics.

Third, you may continue looking through online sources such as financial news releases and stock analysis pieces for new ideas on the companies in the selected investment space. But be sure to take anything with a grain of salt then evaluate both sides of the argument.

Take note that these three methods are by no means the only methods on how you can choose a company, but you can follow them for a quick start. These methods also have their respective benefits and downsides that you must take note.

Looking for companies according to their ETF holdings is possibly the fastest way to filter down your search. But ETFs usually hold only the biggest companies in the space, usually setting aside small capital corporations and micro companies. These forms of funds also have the tendency to concentrate on domestic markets.

Meanwhile, stock screeners are also offering effective ways to filter down the list of firms that are subject for desirable inputs. Even though screeners offer a more exhaustive list of securities that include global companies, the investment metrics uses are usually not that reliable.

Reading expert insights through online sources may take some time, but it carry considerable benefits. At most, reading stock analysis posts will improve your understanding of fundamentals of the industry you are interested to work on. Also, you may also read about small companies that could neither be discovered through ETF holdings or stock screeners.

Explore Company Reports

When you are already convinced that a certain industry is a strong investment and you are already aware of the major players, the next step is to focus your attention to company presentations.

While company presentations are less comprehensive compared to financials, they can provide you a general picture of how companies are making their money and could be easier to explore through compared to 10K or 10Q presentations. Moreover, company reports will typically have a futuristic details on the projected movement of the company as well as its industry.

While the past tips of going through the fund holdings or doing a screen could provide you a considerable number of possible stock investment options, you can still browse around corporate websites and explore their presentation so you can further refine your due diligence. This phase of choosing the stocks to invest in can be more active than the prior stages.

The details that you can obtain from company presentation report includes helpful materials such as overall industry perspective, future opportunities for growth, operational highlights, income statement, cash flow statement, and balance sheet.

Assessing these reports also involve comprehensive analysis of the actual firm so you can decide why a certain stock may outperform other similar stocks. You should know which firms are most enticing according to the available report and filter down your search further. A critical factor to consider is that of course the objective of an investor presentation is to promote the firm.

At this point, you must have at least 10 companies that you want to invest in. Possibly, even after all the time you have placed into looking for a stock, you have realized that the industry doesn't match with your investment goals. This decision is crucial for stock picking because you research has driven a possibly disappointing venture.

If after all the time you spent on research, you are still convinced with your original argument, then your due diligence should move into comprehensive analysis of the company's financials.

Chapter 6 - Forex

The daily fluctuations in the forex market are often very small. Many currency pairs are moving less than 1% every day, which represents a less than 1% movement in the currency value. Hence, we can say that the forex market has low volatility. Most forex speculators are relying on the availability of huge leverage to increase the value of possible fluctuations.

In the retail forex, the leverage could quite high reaching to a maximum of 250 is to 1. This is considered as risky but high liquidity and 24/7 trading enables forex brokers to standardize high leverage to make the movements more profitable for traders.

The availability of high leverage and extreme liquidity have pushed the FX and developed it as an ideal place for most traders. Traders can open and close positions in a span of minutes, days, or even months. Forex prices rely on the objective assessment of the currency demand and supply, and can be extremely difficult to manipulate because of the market size. Even central banks cannot easily move prices at their will.

The forex market is a lucrative ground for traders and investors. But to ensure profitability, a forex trader must understand first the fundamental concepts that drive the fluctuations in the market.

The main objective of this eBook is to provide you a basic foundation before you try forex trading. Never start trading without getting educated first, unless you are willing to learn the trade through experimentation and in the process lose money. In this book, we will cover the fundamentals of exchange rates, jargon, basic concepts you have to understand, and most importantly, proven effective strategies.

When you trade forex you are making money from the fluctuations in value of currencies. Currency values are expressed as exchange rates, in which the price of a currency is defined by how much it can buy of another currency. For instance, a typical currency pair is GBP/USD (UK pound vs. US dollar). For instance, if the GBP/USD exchange rate is 1.245, this means that a pound is worth $1.245.

To illustrate how you make money, let's say the exchange rate moves up to 1.265, or 20 pips (1.265-1.245). If you have a long position of $100,000 then you have made a profit of $2000 (100,000 x .002).

As with stocks, you can also make money by 'short selling' forex, that is, making a bet that the price will go down. In this scenario, if the exchange rate moves down to 1.225 and you have a short position of $100,000, you will make a profit of $2000.

As with stocks, you can also trade forex by using leverage. This will help you greatly magnify your profits, but it will also increase your potential losses. This is why you should use leverage very carefully and determine the appropriate amount to use.

The Forex Spot Market

Basically, the spot market is where you can buy and sell currencies based on the prevailing price. This price, influenced by the current demand and supply, signified different factors such as political situations (global and local), economic performances, prevailing interest rates, and the perception of the performance of the currency pairs. Once you finalize a deal, you refer to it as a spot deal, which is a two-way transaction by which a part will deliver an agreed rate of currency to the other party who will receive the specific amount of another currency at the agreed price of the trade.

When the position is closed, the settlement will be paid in cash. Even though the spot market is referred to as the platform where you can deal with the trade in present, instead of the future, these trades really takes around two to three days before settlement.

Forex Forwards and Futures Markets

Meanwhile in the forwards and the futures markets, you are not actually trading actual currencies. Rather, you deal in contracts that will represent a claim to a certain currency type, a certain unit price. The settlement will be at a future date.

Within the futures FX market, the futures contracts are traded according to a standard size and the date of settlement on public financial markets like the Mercantile Exchange in Chicago. The National Futures Association administers the futures market in the US. The contracts in the futures FX market have certain details that include the units for trade, settlement data, and the price increments. The exchange serves as a representative of the trader to clear and settle the contract.

In the forwards market, on the other hand, the contracts are traded OTC between two parties, who will identify the terms according to their discretion.

Both the forwards and the futures markets are binding are usually settles for cash for the trade in question upon maturity, even though you can still trade the contracts. These markets can provide you protection against risk when you are trading in forex. Global companies are using these commodities to hedge against the rate fluctuations, but speculators are also participating in these markets.

Take note that throughout this book, you will encounter the terms currency market, foreign exchange market, forex, or simply FX. Bear in mind that these terms all mean forex market and so they can be used interchangeably.

In addition, you should learn how to analyze the forex markets. The most commonly used method is technical analysis, which involves looking at historic price data of currencies in order to try and identify future price activity and find trading opportunities. The trading platform that you are provided when you sign up with a forex broker will provide you with a host of tools that you can use to conduct this analysis.

Of course, you should also have a trading plan to ensure that you are trading with discipline. Since forex trading is a short-term activity that involves a lot of price volatility, it is very easy for traders to start getting emotional during trading. This means that there is a risk that you will not close a trade when it starts going against you, thus greatly magnifying your potential losses. Alternately, there is also the risk that you when a trade is going in your favor, you will keep it open for too long and not close it before the price reverses and you start to lose money.

One of the most important things to remember when trading forex is that it is a highly speculative activity, meaning that while you can make money very quickly, you can also lose money just as fast. Thus, you should not enter into forex trading lightly and make sure that you understand how to trade it thoroughly before you make your first trade.

Another way to look into forex trading is to think about your position in taking every currency in the pair. The base currency could be considered as a short position, because you are basically selling this currency to buy the quoted currency that is considered as a long position in the currency pair.

For example, one Canadian dollar can buy $1.1543 and the other way around. To buy Canadian dollars, you must first short the USD so you can go long for the base currency. To make some profit in this investment, you have to sell back the Canadian dollar once its value increases relative to USD.

Getting Started in Forex Trading

The stock market and the forex market have many similarities, but there are some critical differences. This eBook will show you these differences as well as how you can start with forex trading.

How to Choose a Forex Broker

Similar to the stock market, there are many brokers that you can choose to work with in the FX market. Below are several things that you should look for:

Reliable Brokerage Firm

Unlike stock brokers, forex brokers are typically affiliated with lending institutions or big banks because of the huge amounts of capital needed. This amount is usually for the leverage that the broker will be able to provide. In addition, forex brokers are regulated by the CFTC or the Commodity Futures Trading Commission and should be registered with the FCM or the Futures Commission Merchant. You can visit the brokerage firm's website or its parent company's website to look for these information as well as other statistics and details. Make certain that the brokerage you want to work with is affiliated with a credible bank or lending institution.

Low Spreads

The difference between the rate at which a currency could be purchased and the rate at which you can sell it at a certain time is known as the spread. This is calculated in pips. Take note that most brokers are not working on commission as they are making a profit from the spreads. In choosing a broker, you must try to find the difference in spreads. But take note that even if lower spreads can save you money, it is still crucial that you should choose a broker that is reliable.

Leverage Options

Leverage is crucial in the forex market as the profit sources are just a small percentage of a cent. Leverage, written as a ration between the actual capital and the total available capital refers to the amount of money from the broker that you can use for trading. For instance, a 100:1 ratio means that you can use $100 for every dollar in your account. There are also brokerages that offer as high as 250:1. Take note that lower leverage could mean lower risk for a margin call, but may also provide lower value for your money and the other way around. If your capital is limited in your forex account, you can go to a broker who offers high leverage. If capital is not an issue for you, any firm with a range of leverage options can do the job. Access with wide options will allow you extend the risk that you can accept. For instance, lower leverage is ideal for currency pairs that are highly volatile.

Trading Tools and Research

Forex brokerage firms usually provide various trading platforms for their customers, similar to other brokers in the equities markets. These platforms usually feature real-time news and information, tools for technical analysis, real-time charts, and even client support for trading networks. But before you fully sign up, make certain that you have experienced first free trials in order to test various trading platforms. Brokers also offer fundamental and technical insights, economic schedules, and other valuable information. Be sure to choose a broker who can arm you with the tools you need to succeed in this business.

Types of Accounts

Many brokers are offering several account types. The smallest account is referred to as a micro account and usually need you to trade with a minimum of $200. This account usually offer high leverage that you need to make money with initial investment. The standard account will allow you to trade at various leverages, but usually require an initial capital between $1000 and $3000. There are also premium accounts that usually require substantial capital. This allow you to use various leverages and usually provide comprehensive tools and services for trading and research. Be sure that the broker you want to work with is offering the right leverage, services, and tools that is relevant for your capital amount.

Avoid Brokers with Stringent Margin Rules

If you are trading with a borrowed capital, your firm usually has a say in the level of risk that you are taking. Hence, your broker has the discretion to buy or sell, which could negatively affect your trade. For example, let's assume that you are working on a margin account, and your position requires a dive prior to rebounding to all-time highs. In this case, even if you have enough capital to cover the trade, some brokers may choose to liquidate the position on a margin call in this low. This can be costly in your part. Make certain that you review the rules of your chosen broker and find out what other clients are talking about by visiting online forums.

Stay Away from Sniper-Hunters

Sniper-hunters are brokerage firms that are known to buy or sell premature stocks at prior points. These are considered shady practices committed by brokers to bump up their profits. Of course, no brokerage will admit to this practice, and there is no hard and fast rule to determine if the broker is doing this. One way is to talk with fellow traders as there is no organization or blacklist that reports this activity.

Setting up an FX account is pretty much the same as signing up for an equity account. The only difference is that for FX, you need to sign a margin agreement, which states that you need to trade through leverage, and so the broker has the right to intervene with your trade to guard your interests. Upon signing up, you can just fund the account, so you can easily trade.

Establish Your Forex Strategy

Fundamental analysis and technical analysis are two basic categories of strategy in the FX market just like in the stock markets. However, technical analysis is a common strategy used by forex traders.

Among the fundamental concepts of technical analysis is that the future price movement could be predicted by looking into past movements. Because the foreign exchange market is a 24-hour market, you get a chance to assess a huge volume of data, which you can use to measure the price activity, which increases the statistical significance of the projection. Many investors and traders in the forex market are using technical tools like indicators, charts, and trends.

In general, it is crucial to take note that technical analysis interpretation could stay the same regardless of the assets that you are keeping track. In this Chapter, we will discuss the most popular forex strategies based on technical analysis.

Technical Analysis Focuses on the Movement of Trends

In doing technical analysis in the forex market, you need to determine if a currency pair will trend in a specific direction, or if it will remain in the range or go against the trend. A common way to figure out these traits is to place trend lines, which links historical levels that have avoided a rate from going lower or higher. These resistance and support levels are popular among technical traders to find out if the current trend shall continue.

In general, most currency pairs like GBP/USD, USD/CHF, USD/JPY, and EUR/USD have demonstrated the best characteristics of trend, while the currency pairs that have previously demonstrated higher probability to be bounded by range are the currency crosses.

Inconsistency in the Minimal Rate

As we have discussed in the earlier chapter, there are different players in the foreign exchange market such as large banks and hedge funds. These large players are equipped with complex computer systems to continuously keep track of any inconsistencies between the various currency pairs.

With these programs, it can be rare to see any significant inconsistency to last longer than a matter of seconds. Many traders are using technical analysis because it already presumes that all factors that could affect the currency rates such as psychological, social, political, and economic - have already been considered into the present exchange rate by the market.

With many players and with high volume of transactions every day, the trend as well as the capital flow becomes important instead of trying to determine a rate that is mispriced.

Common Indicators in Technical Analysis

Forex traders who prefer technical analysis use various indicators alongside resistance and support levels to help them in projecting the future direction of exchange rates. Take note that learning how to understand different technical indicators is crucial and may require further study on your part.

Among the indicators that you should learn well include stochastics, moving average convergence divergence (MACD), moving averages, Fibonacci retracement, and Bollinger Bands. Take note that these tools are not often used as an independent indicator but rather alongside chart patterns and other indicators.

Fibonacci Indicator

The Fibonacci Indicator is a common indicator used in technical analysis in the forex market. This strategy heavily depend on the pullback and to completely understand how this works, you should revisit your understanding of the forex trend. In looking at every price action separately, it is quite difficult to look for a pattern. Taking a closer look at the larger picture will allow you to identify the trends.

For hundreds of years, the Fibonacci ratios and numbers have been popular among artists and mathematicians. These figures signify many things in mathematics, in nature, and even in the financial markets. Although Fibonacci is a classic concept in mathematics, you don't need to be well adept in the subject so you can use these figures in calculating projections in the forex trading platforms. All you have to do is to make a decision according on the lines that appear on the charts.

Horizontal Levels

Horizontal Levels are among the most simple but quite useful concepts trading in the forex market. These are fundamentals in most forex trading strategies and could help you in studying charts. But you can also use them as a separate strategy instead of a mere tool to ride along with other strategies. In monitoring the most clear-cut price actions and identifying the horizontal levels, you can make profitable trades. In completely becoming familiar with the horizontal levels of advanced charts, you can identify trends that you might have otherwise ignored.

Swing Points

The ideal method in using horizontal levels to your advantage is through the analysis of swing points, which refer to the points where there is a change in trends. By marking the horizontal levels on these places, you can find the prices where there could be a likely change in the trend.

Take note that swing points are more likely to recur themselves. Resistance levels could turn into support levels, and the other way around. When you mark the horizontal levels on your graph, you could project the next point of the swing will likely to happen and exit or enter a trade at the right time.

Ranging Markets

Horizontal levels can be used in ranging markets, which refers to the condition in which the price has clear lower and upper boundaries. By monitoring the price when it is approaching a limit, you can project with precision the points where the price could be more likely to next continue the trend.

It can be hard to predict the price, and may even break down the boundary as you are deciding to enter the trade. But in general, this forex technical strategy is safe and very reliable.

Divergence

Traders as well as analysts of financial markets, aside from the market fundamentals, are using several indicators to determine what could happen to the price of a specific instrument. These indicators will provide you a basic method of recognizing patterns and projecting which way the price could trend. Using these indicators is what makes signals in the forex market helpful, as you can use them for real-time analysis of the price action.

Divergence is one such indicator, which can help you to significantly increase your profits in the forex market. The probability of entering in the correct direction at the right time could increase if you use this indicator alongside other indicators such as support and resistance levels, stochastics, RSI, and moving averages.

Fundamental Analysis

In the stock market, fundamental analysis measures the true value of a company. A fundamentalist (one who mainly use fundamental analysis) base his decision to invest or trade in stocks according to the calculation.

Somehow, this is similar in the foreign exchange market, where fundamentalists are also looking into the true value of the countries and their currencies. They are also watching out for economic announcements in order to gain an idea of the true value of the currency.

In general, geo-political events, economic data, and news reports from a certain country are regarded similarly to announcements about stocks and companies used by investors to gain insight of their true value. The value may change over time because of several factors including financial strength and growth. Fundamentalists are focusing on this data to assess the currency of the countries in the currency pair that he is interested in.

In this Chapter, we will discuss the top forex fundamental strategies that are used by traders and investors today.

Forex Carry Trade

The forex carry trade is an investment strategy wherein a trader is offering a currency that has lower interest rates and buys a currency with higher interest rate. To put it simply, you are lending currencies at a higher rate and borrow at a lower rate. In using this strategy, you can make profits through the difference between these two rates.

Remember, when you are leveraging a trade, even a slight movement between the rates could result to great profits or great losses. Aside from capturing the differences on the rates, the traders also focuses on the increasing value of the currency, because money flows into the currency that is high-yielding that increases its value,

One good example of this is the carry trade of the Japanese yen in 1999, when the country lowered down its interest rates to almost 0%. Investors eventually capitalized on these lower interest rates by borrowing substantial amount of Japanese yen, which was converted into USD to purchase US treasury bonds. These bonds guaranteed as high as 5%. Because the Japanese interest rate was basically zero, the investors are not paying any substantial amount to borrow yen and made a lot of profit from the US treasury bonds. Through proper leverage, you can substantially increase your profits in forex trading.

For instance, a 20 times leverage will yield a return of 30% on a 3% yield. If you have $500 in your account and you have access to 20 times leverage, you can control $10,500. If you try the carry trade strategy from our example, you can earn 3% per annum. By the year-end, your $10,000 investment will be $10300. Take note that you have only invested $1,000 from your pocket, so your actual return is 30%.

But bear in mind that this strategy is only applicable if the value of the currency pair appreciates or not changing. Hence, many forex traders who are using the carry trade strategy focus not only on earning from the interest of the difference between the interest rates, but also for appreciating capital. For the sake of giving simple examples, we have simplified the transactions given here. It is crucial to take note that there is a minimal difference in interest rate that could lead to huge gains when you apply the leverage. Many forex brokers need a small margin for earning interest rates for implementing the carry trade strategy.

Trading the News

Significant news events around the world could have a large impact on the foreign exchange market, which usually render all analysis meaningless. Take note that the forex market is a 24-hour market, and there is no way to schedule the announcement of news. Changes in the market according on the economy and data could hit any type of trader wherever you are and whichever currency you choose to trade.

If you are in Europe and you want to trade Swiss Francs, you can always read news from Europe. If you prefer Yen or Yuan, then you have to watch for news from Japan, China, and Asia in General. Same goes for other currencies. You have to check the news every day to be updated on any information that could affect your trading.

In the equities market, significant news are often about the publication of corporate earnings, profits, macroeconomic data, profits per share, etc. In the forex market, significant news that affects the market can be announcements from the Central Banks, political events, economic news, inflation reports, and more.

Among the first lessons for beginners in the forex market is when trading, you must be careful in the market during significant news announcements. Nonetheless, you may still find yourself trading during the news, and usually it is not because of being selfish or greedy. Some traders just like the feeling of excitement or adrenaline rush. Some are addicted to the thrill, but most forex traders are only after the profits. After all, you are mainly trading for profits, and the risk is a natural part of the process.

There are always two currencies involved in forex trading. If you are planning to open a position, the news from the two countries must be taken into consideration alongside other foreign news that may affect the currency pair.

For instance, if your decide to trade CHF/NZD, aside from assessing the possible results of the news from Switzerland and New Zealand, and the effect that it could have on the pair, you should also consider significant news from Europe and Asia or anywhere because the news may cause any movement in the financial markets. If there was really good economic data from Australasia, the pair will rally because it means that demand for European products may likely to follow an upward trend. The opposite may happen if the economic conditions in Europe are not that strong. It could affect the worldwide financial market and the traders may likely choose currency alternatives such as USD and Yen.

Short Term News Trading

Short term news trading is a bit more challenging because of the volatility as well as the tighter stops. More often than not, minutes before and after, there are whipsaws with the rate frantically moving in both directions. Short term news trading is also divided into several strategies:

One method is to sell the currency spike after a bad news. There are instances that even after bad announcements, the price slightly increases for several seconds or even minutes. This is the best time to sell, particularly if it is at some significant resistance or level.

On the other hand, buying after bad news, because of past good data may cause a currency pair to form an uptrend. Even though infrequent, worse than expected news should not be ignored, although this will not affect the general outlook of the situation. Hence, after an initial fall, you should look to buy the immediate response from the market.

Long Term News Trading

When looking for long-term trading opportunities according on economic news, it is crucial to assess both the previous and current data. This is because there are instances that news may take weeks or months to be significantly absorbed by the market. You can use the information to see a larger picture and the impact that it may have on the currency you want to trade. The long term trends are built by fundamental factors that are founded on numerous economic pieces over a specific period of time.

For example, the currency pair GBP/USD started on an uptrend a year ago, and it continued ever since. On the other hand, EUR/GBP is following a falling trend for some time now. Take note that these trends have not started out right after.

Market Sentiment

By now, you already understand that trading in the forex market can be difficult especially for beginners. Market sentiment refers to the momentum of the market. All forex traders have their own style in trading - some may be bearish, and some may be bullish. Hence, market sentiment is the style of the different traders combined, which produces the general condition of the market.

There are instances that every indicator is pointing in a specific direction but the market is moving in the opposite. There are instances that the fundamental condition of the economy can be considered as bearish for a particular currency, and nevertheless, it keeps on fluctuating upwards in comparison with other currencies.

One example of this is the high movement of the USD/EUR that started in 2012 until early 2017. The European economy in general was not progressing with many member countries still suffering the effects of the recession, inflation falling, and political unrest in some countries. In the US, the economy was recovering in spite of the fair conditions in Europe, the currency pair still rises to an average of 1.40.

It is important that forex beginners be familiar with the market sentiment. Not only will it let you read the market sentiment in general, but you can also successfully trade and make profits not only in the foreign exchange market but also in other commodities as well. More often than not, the market sentiment is easy to analyze, because you only need to focus on the primary trend of a particular pair such as the good trend in EUR/USD between 2012 and 2014.

How to Read the Market Sentiment

You will surely encounter some tips on forex trading on the importance of the trend as an indicator in forex trading. Somehow, this is true as the trend will allow you to find out the market sentiment. But there are times that trends can be difficult to read. For instance, a day trader who trades every 15 minutes to one hour, may see the trend pointing in single trend. But hours later, the trend may change and so you can lose money.

Trends can really change fast. The larger the trend within the daily or four-hour chart could have been trending in the opposing direction, and so the trend that a day trader might be looking at could just be the larger trend's correction. Therefore, before you can place an order based on a lower chart timeframe, you need to check first the charts that cover a wider timeframe. Through this, you will be able to sense the market sentiment and find the pairs you can position your bets on.

Price Action

Focusing on a single currency pair one at a time is a good way to be familiar with the general market sentiment. Through this, you can gradually master reading currency pairs. Many lucrative forex traders are successfully trading according on their price action sense. In this strategy, you must keep track how quick a specific pair is moving in the two directions.

How to Set-up Your Forex Trading Account and Begin Trading

At this point, you may feel that you can now begin to trade in the foreign exchange market. Make sure that you understand this Chapter so you can learn the important steps to set-up forex account and then begin trading currencies. We will also include other important considerations that you must understand before you open up your forex trading account.

Setting Up a Forex Trading Account

Forex trading is quite similar to stock market trading because you have to open a trading account first. Similar to the stock market, every forex account as well as the services you can take advantage of can be different. Hence, it is crucial that you look for the most suitable platform for you. In this Chapter, we will discuss the important factors that you consider when you are choosing a foreign exchange account.

Trading Leverage

When we speak of leverage, we refer to the opportunity to take control of bigger amounts of cash with minimal capital from your own pocket. The leverage level is directly proportional to the risk level. Take note that the leverage amount on a platform could be different according to the features of the account on its own. However, the most popular one is the 50:1 leverage, and some accounts could even offer a maximum leverage of 250:1.

For example, a maximum leverage of 100:1 signifies that with each dollar you hold in the brokerage account, you can use up to $100 for trading. For instance, if you have an account balance of $100, the brokerage can allow you to trade as much as $10,000 in the FX. This leverage could also define the total amount that you can hold in your account or your margin for trading a specific amount. In the stock market, the margin is often at 50 per cent and the leverage could be 50:1, which can be at least 2 per cent.

In general, leverage is regarded as a primary advantage of trading in the foreign exchange market, because this will allow you to create substantial gains with minimal capital. But leverage could also have extreme downsides when a trade is moving in the opposite direction, because the losses could also be big.

With this leverage type, there is always the actual probability that your losses are higher than what you have invested, even though most accounts have safeguard stops to prevent the account from hitting negative. As such, it is crucial that you take note of this when you open a brokerage account, and once you identify your preferred leverage, you could understand the involved risks more.

Fees and Commissions

Another major advantage of forex platforms is that investing through them could be done through a commission, which is unlike stock market accounts where you need to pay a broker a certain fee for every trade. You are now directly dealing with market players and you don't have to pass through another layer such as brokers.

Every time that you enter a trade, it is the market makers, which can seize the spread. Hence, when the ask/bid for a forex market is 1.5300/50, the market maker can capture between the difference between the points.

In setting up your own forex account, be sure to take note that every firm has various spreads on currency pairs that you trade. Even though they are usually different by only several pips, this could be substantial when you are planning to do a lot of trading. Hence, in setting up an account, be certain that you are aware of the pip and spread of specific currency pairs that you are interested in trading.

Other Factors

You must take note that there are several differences between every forex platform and the programs or software that they are offering. Hence, it is crucial to review every firm before you make a commitment. Every forex trading company may offer various levels of programs and services including the fees beyond and above the actual costs of trading. Moreover, because of the less strict conditions in the foreign exchange market, you should find a reliable firm. When you are also not completely confident to trade with real cash, you can also try trading in practice accounts or demos.

How to Start Trading in the Forex Market

After understanding the most crucial factors in opening your own forex account, it is time to look into what specifically you could trade within the platform. The two primary methods in trading in the forex market includes the actual trading (selling and buying) of forex pairs, in which you short a currency and long another. Another method is via buying the derivatives that monitor the fluctuations of particular currency pair. These strategies are quite similar to the common techniques used in the stock market. Basically, buying and selling the currency pair is the most popular method, much in a similar manner that many traders are buying and selling currency units.

In this setting, a trader may hope that the currency pair's value will change in a profitable way. If you choose to short a pair, it signifies that you are betting on the possibility that the pair's value will fall. For instance, let's assume that you want a short position for the USD/JPY pair. You can make profits when the value of the FX pair goes down, and you will lose your investment if it rises. This pair will rise if USD increases its price against the JPY, therefore it is actually a trust on the JPY.

Another alternative is to use futures and options, which are derivative products, so you can make money from the currency value changes. If you purchase a currency pair option, you can gain the privilege to buy a pair on a specific rate prior to a setting of point. Meanwhile, a futures forex contract could build the agreement to purchase the currency pair at a specific point. These trading strategies are often employed by more experienced traders, but as a beginner, you should be at aware of them.

Order Types

When looking for a new trading position, you might need to use a market or limit order, which are actually similar when placing a new position in the stock market. A market order can provide you the capacity to acquire the currency at specific exchange rate that it is presently trading in the foreign exchange market. On the other hand, the limit order will allow you to identify a specific entry price.

If you are already holding an open position in the market, you may consider employing a take profit order, so you could lock in your gains. For instance, let us assume that you are already sure that the USD/GBP will react at 1.8700, but you are not completely certain that the price will rise any higher. You can use a take-profit order that will immediately close your position if the price hits 1.8700, which will lock in your profits.

The stop loss order is also a tool that you can use when you want to hold the open positions. This will allow you to figure out if the price could decline prior to the closing of the position and more losses could be accumulated. Hence, if the USD/GBP rate starts to drop, the investor may put a stop-loss, which could halt the position to avoid any further loss.

When you are also trading in the stock market, you will realize that the order types that you could enter in the forex trading accounts are quite similar. It is crucial to be familiar with these orders before you actually place your very first trade in the foreign exchange market.

Chapter 7 - Precious Metals

Precious metals, gold in particular, are among the most popular investment assets. Gold has long been used as a standard on which to fix the value of currency, and has thus gained a reputation as a good long-term investment. Gold is seen to hold its value over time, and thus, provides a valuable hedge against inflation. You can invest a certain amount in the metal and be assured that when you eventually sell it, it will still be worth the equivalent value.

Gold is a highly-valued precious metal because of its ability to conduct electricity and heat, malleability, and durability. It is also used in electronics and dentistry, but it is more popular as a form of currency and as the base metal for jewelry.

The value of this precious metal is based on the market 24 hours a day and seven days a week. It is interesting to note that gold is traded mainly through the sentiment of the market because its price is not heavily affected by the laws of demand and supply. Even if there are new mines discovered, it may not be enough to have a substantial effect on the volume of gold already in circulation or in stock. Basically, if the market wants to sell its gold, the price may drop, and if they like to buy, the new supply can be immediately absorbed in the market that can drive the price of gold upwards.

There are several factors that increases the desirability of hoarding gold:

1. Inflation – If the real rates of return in the real estate, bond, or equity markets are not positive, people usually hold into gold as an asset, which has the ability to maintain its value.
2. Systemic Financial Conditions – Gold is also used as a storage of value when the banking and currency systems are perceived as not stable
3. Political Instability – Political instability, including war or civil unrest, have always influence people to hoard gold more. A lifetime savings could be stored through gold and can be traded back again for currency to buy food or a new home in a safe location.

One of the reasons why gold retains its value is because there is only a finite quantity of it available, with annual production adding only a relatively small amount to the supply every year. Thus, the price of gold is mainly determined by changes in demand, rather than supply. Gold remains in high demand not only due to its use in jewelry production, but also since it has industrial uses. There is little risk that the supply of gold will suddenly go up due to surges in production. Compare this to currencies, whose values are constantly under pressure due to governments pumping more money into their economies to address fiscal deficits.

Investors in physical gold usually buy them either as gold bars (bullion) or as coins (currency). Alternately, investors who would like exposure to gold without actually having to take possession of the physical metal can buy exchange-traded products such as exchange-traded funds and notes. An ETF holds gold and then allows investors to buy shares in the fund. These shares can be traded as if they were stocks or other financial instruments.

Silver

Not similar to gold, silver's price may fluctuate between its perceived role as value for storage and its role in industrial application. Hence, the price of this precious metal is more volatile compared to gold.

Hence, while silver can be traded in line with gold as a value that can be hoarded depending on the demand, the supply factor for industrial application can also have more dynamic impact on the price. This equation may fluctuate with new innovations such as silver's role in production of microcircuits, superconductors, and batteries. Another important factor was the emergence of middle class in the market economies in Asia that resulted to an explosive demand for medical products, electrical appliances, and other industrial items that require silver.

Platinum

Similar to silver and gold, platinum is also a precious metal that is traded around the globe every day. It has the tendency to carry a higher price more than gold during political stability, mainly because there is a limited supply. Below are the other factors that influence the price of this metal:

1. Platinum mines are located in only two countries: Russia and South Africa. This also creates better potential for cartel-like action that could support or even influence the price of platinum.
2. Platinum is also regarded as an industrial metal, and its highest demand comes from manufacturers of catalytic converters that cars use to lessen carbon emission. This precious metal is also used in jewelries and in refining petroleum products.
3. Because of the car industry's heavy dependence on the metal, platinum prices can be determined in substantial part by auto sales as well as number of production. The push for clean air regulations also mandate automakers to add more catalytic converters that rises in demand. Car makers also began using recycled catalysts or using more palladium, which has similar properties to platinum but less expensive and more stable.

Take note that these factors serve to make platinum a highly volatile precious metal. Hence, it can be ideal to have some investment in platinum, but don't place all your money in this.

How Can You Invest in Precious Metals

Below are the options available if you like to invest in precious metals.

Mutual Funds and Common Stocks

The price movements of precious metals are leveraged by the shares of miners of precious metals. Unless you are fully aware of the valuation of mining stocks, it is wiser to follow funds with managers with outstanding performance track.

Precious Metals ETFs

ETFs are available for gold, silver, and platinum. Investing into these ETFs is a convenient way to buy and sell precious metals.

Options and Futures

The options and futures markets provide liquidity and leverage to investors who like to place large bets on precious metals. The best potential profits and losses that you can obtain from market derivatives.

Certificates

Certificates will provide you with all the advantages of owning actual gold without the hassle of storage and transportation. Hence, if you are looking to cover risk during natural disasters, certificates are only documents, and no one can steal them as they are under your name.

Bars and Coins

Physical gold, silver, or platinum are ideal for those who have space to store them. If you have a time horizon, physical possession of precious metals may not be ideal as they can be bothersome to hold and they are not that easy to sell in the open market.

Investing in precious metals can protect you from inflation. They are exempted from inflation as it is impossible to manufacture them, they don't have any credit risk, and they have intrinsic value. They also provide genuine insurance against military, political, or financial upheavals.

In an investment perspective, precious metals can offer negative or low correlation to other classes of assets such as bonds and stocks. Hence, even a minor percentage of precious metals in your investment portfolio will lessen risk and volatility.

Precious metals offer a valuable and efficient way to diversify your portfolio. The key in achieving success in this investment is to determine your goals and risk profile before you buy anything. Precious metals have high volatility, which you can harness to gain wealth, but it could damage your investment if not managed well.

Other investment analysts recommend investing in silver rather than gold. They argue that while gold has gotten the bulk of investors' attention, silver provides just as many advantages. Silver is more widely used in industry than gold, and thus, demand for it would continue to be high, even over the long-term. However, since silver is more accessible than gold, you can buy it at a lower price and it would still fulfill its function as a store of wealth.

In addition, some analysts believe that the price of silver is due to go up due to a correction in the ratio of gold-to-silver. At present, the ratio is around 1:60, meaning that an ounce of gold is equivalent to sixty ounces of silver. This ratio is seen to eventually move back to its average historical level of 1:15. If this happens, then silver would become more valuable, since less of it is needed to buy its equivalent in gold.

If you were interested in investing in precious metals, the best use for them would be to protect your one million nest egg against inflation. You can hold a certain percentage of the million in gold or silver to ensure that it will not be devalued by inflation when you have to liquidate it in the future.

PART III

WRITING YOUR ONE-YEAR INVESTMENT PLAN

Chapter 8 - How to Write an Investment Plan

Writing a simple investment plan is not always easy. Even though the fundamentals of smart investing can be straightforward, implementing these strategies could be difficult. This is mainly because we tend to be emotional. Most people are frightened if the market conditions are bad and they are tempted to sell. On the other hand, greed may come forward if the market is doing well.

The best way to lessen the effect of emotion in investing is to build your own investment plan. An investment plan every year will drastically simplify your decision making and will make your investment more lucrative.

In this Chapter, we will discuss how you can write a plan for one year. You must be able to use this plan at times of market crashes so you can stay on track. In this process, we will use my friends Allan & Judy who I have helped in building their investment document.

The Fundamentals

Objectives

In the objectives section, you must clearly describe your investment objectives as well as timeline. As with most investors, retirement is a main investment objective for Allan and Judy. The specific objective is to earn $1 million in a retirement portfolio at the end of the year, which is a number that they have arrived after comprehensive discussion about their sources of income, risk profile, and other important factors.

Another typical investment objective is to pay for college. Allan and Judy have one child that they are expecting to send to college in the next five years. Their goal is to save $100,000 for their son's college fund. This amount was determined by getting the estimate on how much college may likely cost by the time that their son is ready for college.

Portfolios and accounts

The next step is to describe which funds are allocated for each objective. I would often recommend several accounts, which are designed for the same purpose as a part of one account. For instance, Allan and Judy's retirement fund can be composed of three accounts: Allan's IRA, Judy's IRA, and Allan's 401(k). This strategy of looking at individual accounts as one category will make the allocation of assets a lot easier, and this is normally affordable, because every recommended fund only requires to be purchased once rather than once in every separate account.

However, college funds are quite different. The child's account requires a personalized investment. Even though the objective of every account can be the same, the age of the child mean that the allocation and approach could be different.

Investment Strategy

In this section, you should describe the investment methodology that you have selected for every portfolio. Also include your strategy if you are investing into real estate. Are you willing to do house-flipping, or you want rental income? You should also have a separate strategy for your investment in stocks, forex, and precious metals.

Asset Allocation

Asset allocation is at the core of the investment process. As an investor, you must ground the decision-making structure on solid foundation of long-term actions. By concentrating on asset allocation, you can relegate security selection and market timing, which can reduce the level of investment results on unstable factors.

A good way to measure your risk tolerance and losses is to take a risk tolerance test to determine how you will likely respond in different settings. By taking a closer look at the performance of specific asset allocation strategies, you could determine how the gains and losses over these cycles will have made you feel. You may gain a better handle on your investment decisions and emotions if similar conditions happen in the future.

Contributions

Be sure to write down how much you are willing to contribute every month on every account. It is ideal that these contributions are set up on automatic arrangements. For instance, you may allocate 20% of your salary to your 401(k) plan. This requires review of your income sources as well as your expenses.

Rebalancing

This portion describes how often you want to rebalance your portfolio. It is ideal to rebalance your accounts before the year ends or at the start of the year.

Chapter 9 - Your One-Year Investment Plan

Below is a sample investment plan that you may follow to start earning 1 million in 1 year.

January

Start the journey by reviewing your overall finances. Revisit your income sources, take a closer look at your portfolio, and determine how much you need to earn your goal of earning $1 million in one year. It is ideal to consult a licensed financial advisor or financial planner to help you out in the process. At the end of this month, you should have a polished investment plan.

February

The first quarter of this year should be allocated to learning real estate investments. Most people who have made a million dollars in one year have large investments in real estate. For this month, you should devote your time and resources in learning about real estate. The expected result for this month is that you have finally chosen your real estate investment strategy and you have already sourced out the funds you need for this venture.

March

By this month, you should have started your real estate investment strategy. If you have chosen house flipping, you should have already found a good house to flip. And if you prefer a rental property, you should have already found a place that can yield your stable rental income.

April

At this point, you should already have a real estate investment that is giving your regular income. Be sure that at this 2nd quarter of the year, your real estate venture is already stable, so you can open up yourself to learn a new form of investment - the stock market. Devote enough time and resources to learn how the equities market work, and be sure that you are armed with the right knowledge and skills before you buy stocks.

May

By this month, you should already into stock investing. It is ideal that you have at leads 10 to 15 stocks in your portfolio from diverse industries. You should work with a mutual fund manager so you can still have time to manage your real estate business.

June

This month should be devoted into two major things. First, revisit your real estate investment if it is giving you the expected income. Second, review your stock investment to make sure that you are holding the right stocks poised for growth. You must set aside time to do a mid-year performance review and try to figure out if you can actually hit your target. Make some changes at this point depending on the results of your investment in real estate and in the equities market.

July

If you have determined that you are in the right track, which means your real estate investment and stocks are doing well. You should start adding a new form of investment - forex market. Devote enough time and resources to learn how the forex market work, and be sure that you are armed with the right knowledge and skills before you buy currency pairs.

August

By this month, you should already know the fundamentals of forex investments.
It is ideal that you have at leads 5 currency pairs in your portfolio. You should work with a forex manager so you can still have time to manage your real estate business and stocks investments.

September

This month should be devoted into three major things. First, revisit your real estate investment if it is giving you the expected income. Second, review your stock investment to make sure that you are holding the right stocks poised for growth. Third, determine if your forex investments are performing as expected.

You must set aside time to do another performance review and try to figure out if you can actually hit your target.

October

In this last quarter of the year, you should already have the following investments in your portfolio: real estate, stocks, and forex. If you are doing well in these investments and if you have enough resources, you should add precious metals in your portfolio. Take note that precious metals are exempted from inflation, so they can reduce the risk of losing your investments if you add them into your portfolio.

November

At this point, you should already have chosen precious metals and added them into your portfolio. Be sure to choose the right method of investing into gold, silver or platinum. You may choose ETFs, certificates, or buy actual precious metals and store them physically within your premises.

December

Hopefully before the end of the year, you have already accumulated investments and assets that are worth $1 million. At this point, you should try to rebalance your account to make sure that they will perform as expected.

Month	Investment	Expected Yield
January	Planning Stage	
February	Real Estate	90% to 110% (house flipping)
March	Real Estate	90% to 110% (house flipping)
April	Stock Market	6% p.a.
May	Stock Market	6% p.a.
June	Stock Market	6% p.a.
July	Forex	4% p.m.
August	Forex	4% p.m.
September	Forex	4% p.m.
October	Precious Metals	2% p.a.
November	Precious Metals	2% p.a.
December	Rebalancing	

Conclusion

Together, we have explored some of the ways that you could make a million dollars in one year. Although it is possible to do so, I advise you to try to grow your money more gradually rather than attempting to achieve this goal in a relatively short amount of time.

Trying to do so may cause you to take on a higher level of risk in your investments than you would normally find acceptable, which could cause you to lose your investment capital. Still, if you are determined to try to make a million in a year, make sure that you have a solid investment plan and that you are disciplined in following it.